Table of Contents

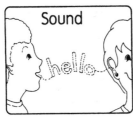

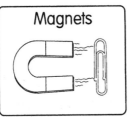

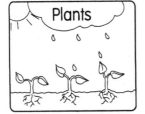

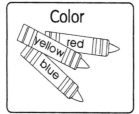

Hands-On Science

Introduction

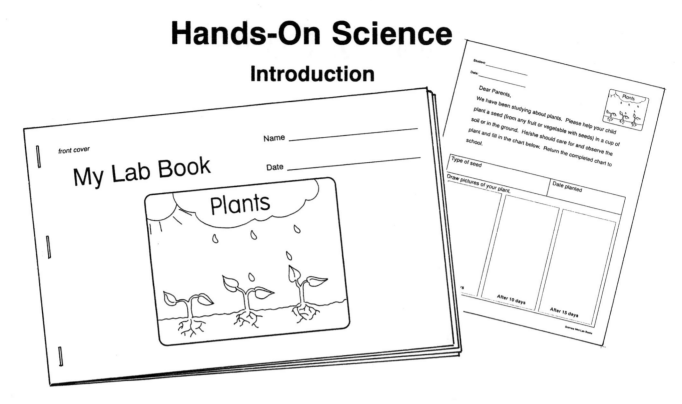

Teachers know that children are most interested in their learning and learn most effectively when they are actively involved. One way to get children actively involved is through the use of manipulative materials. The primary goal of this science program is to enhance student learning by providing activities that will stimulate student interest through a direct, hands-on approach.

The lessons in these "mini-lab books" are intended to be used with children in grades one through three and are designed for use in the classroom throughout the entire school year. These lessons emphasize an active and problem-solving approach to learning which can be teacher directed or carried out by individuals or small groups of children working cooperatively. Each lab book contains a follow-up independent study activity.

The design of these lab book lessons provides for ease and continuity in teaching for the beginning as well as the more experienced teacher. The lessons use common everyday materials which can easily be found, obtained free, or purchased rather inexpensively. These lessons can be used as separate units or to supplement any existing science program.

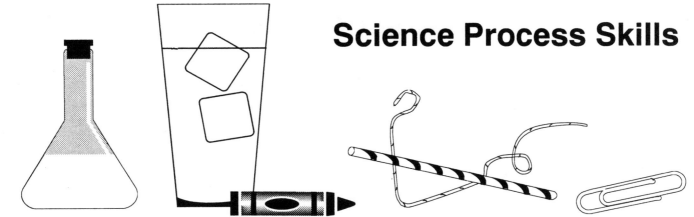

Science Process Skills

The following science process skills are contained in these science lessons:

1. **Observing** is the use of one or more of the five senses to identify and describe the properties of objects or events.

2. **Classifying** is sorting, grouping, labeling, and ordering.

3. **Measuring** is finding out the size, quantity, and/or other properties of an object by comparing the object with a standard.

4. **Predicting** is forecasting what future observations may occur.

5. **Inferring** is explaining an observation. Inferences require evaluations, judgments, and/or speculations on the part of the observer.

6. **Recording** is writing information.

Instruction Design

The clinical instruction design can easily be incorporated into these lessons:

Anticipatory Set:
- stating the objective
- transfer from previous lesson
- content of lesson

Instruction:
- motivation
- reinforcement
- monitoring and adjusting
- higher level thinking skills
- interest level
- immediate knowledge of results

Guided Practice:
- all students involved
- teacher makes adjustment
- specific knowledge of results

Independent Practice:
- mass practice - distributed practice
- monitoring of learner

Closure:
- has the objective been met?
- students demonstrate that learning has taken place

Science Units

January	February	March	April
May	June	July	August
September	October	November	December

Hands-On-Science

Hands-On-Science

Aquarium

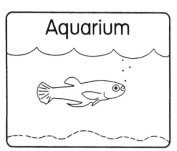

Aquarium

Objectives:

The student will learn:

1. The characteristics of living things.
2. That structures help fish adapt to their environment.
3. Temperature is important in maintaining a stable environment.

Materials to use with student lab books:

Page 1:
- fish tank with two molly fish
- male and female swordtail fish
- catfish
- African frog
- thermometer

Page 4:
- magnifying glass

Page 5:
- picture or diagram which shows the parts of a fish

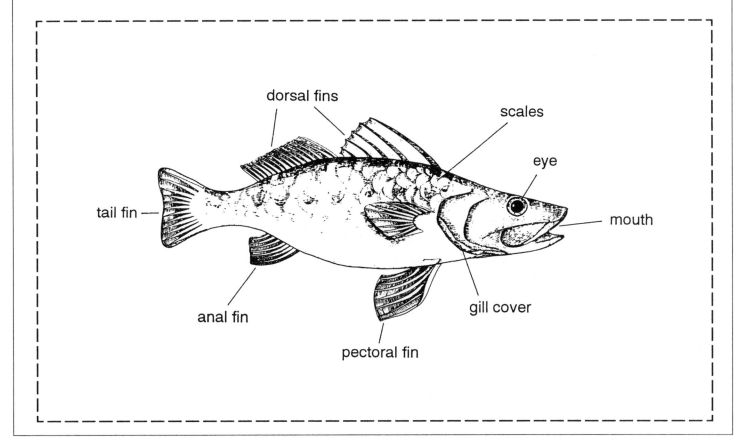

front cover

My Lab Book

Name _____

Date _____

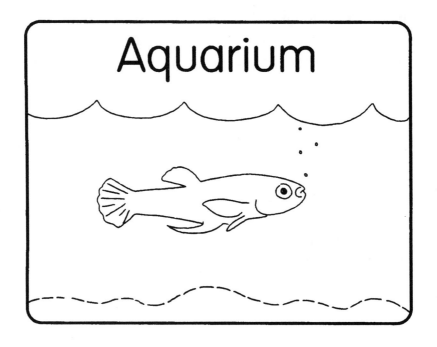

- -

back cover

Three things I've learned about aquariums:

1. _____

2. _____

3. _____

Page 1

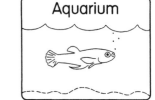

Aquarium

1. There are _____ fish in the fish tank.

2. There are _____ molly fish.

3. There are _____ swordtail fish.

4. There is/are _____ catfish.

5. The water temperature is _____ degrees.

6. Write 3 words that tell how a fish would feel if you could touch it.

   _____ _____ _____

7. Do you think the fish get bored? _____

   Why? _____

- -

Page 2

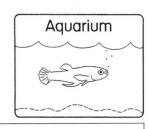

Aquarium

Draw and color a molly fish.	Draw and color the catfish.

Page 3

Draw and color a male and female swordtail fish.

Male   Female

Aquarium

Page 4

Use a magnifying glass. Draw a picture of a fish.
Show how the skin looks.

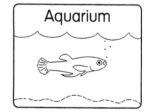

Aquarium

Page 5

Draw a large picture of a fish. Label its parts.
Use a book, picture, or diagram to help you.

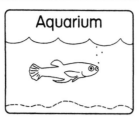

Aquarium

Page 6

1. Draw and color the African frog.

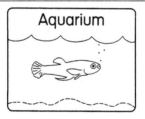

Aquarium

2. Do you think it could hop out? _____

3. Can it live out of water? _____

         Hands-On Science

Page 7

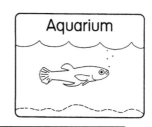

Aquarium

1. Do the fish sleep? _____

2. Do the fish blink their eyes? _____

3. What helps the fish move? _____

4. Can fish move backwards? _____

5. Do the fish see in front? _____

6. How do the fish breathe? _____

7. Do fish take care of their babies? _____

8. How can we help protect the babies? _____

_____

- -

Page 8

Aquarium

Draw the aquarium, fish and their environment.

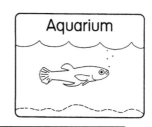

Student: _____

Date: _____

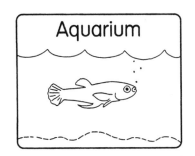

Aquarium

Dear Parents,

We have been studying about fish and their environment. Please help your child find a book, visit a pet store or visit a friend who has an aquarium. Have your child use this page to draw a picture of three or more fresh-water fish in their environment. Have your child bring his/her drawing to share with the class.

Sincerely,

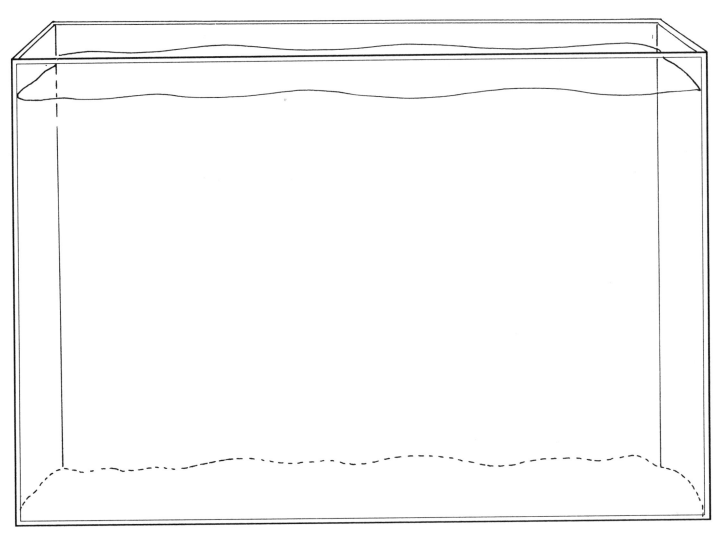

Hands-On Science

Hands-On-Science

Sound

Objectives:

The student will learn that:
1. Vibrations produce sound.
2. Sound travels through things.
3. Solids are better conductors of sound than air.
4. Sounds may be loud, soft, high, low, pleasant, or harsh.

Materials to use with student lab books:

Page 1:
• wooden ruler

Page 2:
• large cup
• rubber band

Page 3:
• small piece of paper

Page 4:
• paper plate
• uncooked rice
• radio or tape recorder

Page 6:
• paper towel tube
• paper, towel or cloth

Page 7:
• ticking watch or clock

Page 8:
• string
• paper cups

Page 9:
• six prepared bottles*
  of colored water

Page 10:
• crayons

Helpful Hints:

When making a string telephone, tie a paper clip in the knot to prevent the string from pulling out.

*Preparation of bottles: You'll need food coloring, water, and six soda bottles the same size. Fill 1/6 of the first bottle with water and add 1 drop of red food coloring. Fill 1/3 of the second bottle with water and add 1 drop of red and 1 drop of blue coloring. Fill 1/2 of the third bottle with water and add 2 drops of blue coloring. Fill 2/3 of the fourth bottle with water and add 2 drops of yellow and 2 drops of blue coloring. Fill 5/6 of the fifth bottle with water and add 3 drops of yellow coloring. Fill the last bottle full of water and add 2 drops of yellow and 2 drops of red coloring.

 Hands-On Science

My Lab Book

Name _____

Date _____

Sound

hello

- -

back cover

Three things I've learned about sound:

1. _____

2. _____

3. _____

Page 1

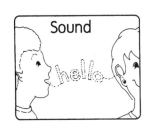

Sound

1. Lay a wooden ruler on the table so that most of it hangs over the edge.

2. Hold the end down on the table, press down hard on the free end, and let it go suddenly.

3. What do you hear? _____

4. Notice how the ruler moves up and down as a sound is made. We say that the ruler is _____.

- -

Page 2

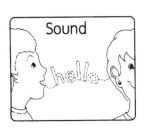

Sound

1. Place a rubber band around the cup from top to bottom.

2. Place your ear next to the cup. What do you hear?

   _____

3. Now, pluck the rubber band with your finger.

4. Do you hear something? _____

5. In order to make sound, what must the rubber band do?

   _____

6. This back-and-forth motion is called _____.

7. Use your cup with the rubber band to complete the following page.

 Hands-On Science

Page 3

1. Choose a partner.

2. While one partner plucks the rubber band, the other partner touches the rubber band with a piece of paper.

3. What do you hear? _____

4. What caused the paper to vibrate and make sound?

   _____

   _____

5. Can we transfer the vibration from a rubber band to a piece of paper? _____

- -

Page 4

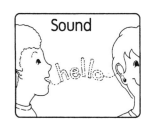

1. Put some rice on a paper plate.

2. Put the plate on a radio.

3. Turn on the radio. What happens to the rice? _____

   _____

4. Why? _____

   _____

5. Can you feel the radio vibrating if you touch it? _____

6. If you turn off the radio, will the rice keep moving? _____

18   Hands-On Science

Page 5

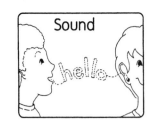
Sound

1. You make sounds when you talk or hum.

   Do you vibrate? _____

2. Place your hand on your throat and hum.

   Do you feel vibrations? _____

3. What do you think is vibrating? _____

   _____

4. When you whistle, do your vocal cords vibrate? _____

5. What is it that is vibrating?_____

Page 6

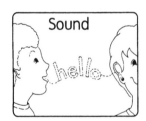
Sound

1. Talk into one end of a paper towel tube.

2. Does sound travel through air? _____

3. Cover one end of the tube with paper.

   Talk into the open end of the tube.

4. Does sound travel through paper? _____

5. Cover one end of the tube with a towel.

   Talk into the open end of the tube.

6. Does sound travel through the towel? _____

Page 7

1. Let's find out if sound can travel through a table.

2. If I stand at one end of the table holding my watch and you stand at the other end, will you hear the watch ticking?_____

3. Now I will place the watch on the table and you put your ear on the top of your end of the table.

4. Do you hear the watch ticking now? _____

5. Which is the better sound conductor:

    air (a gas)_____

    table (a solid) _____

Page 8

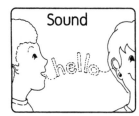

1. Do you think sound will travel through a string? _____

2. Choose a partner.

3. Stretch out a piece of string.

4. Pluck the string and listen.

5. Do you hear any sound? _____

6. We can improve the way the string delivers sound by adding cups to each end.

7. Make a string telephone using your string and paper cups.

Page 9

1. Blow across the top of the bottles.

2. How many different sounds can you hear? _____

3. Which bottle makes the highest sound? _____

4. Which bottle makes the lowest sound? _____

5. Tap the bottles with a metal spoon.

6. Experiment with the different sounds.

7. Make up your own tune.

8. Keep a record of your tune so you can read and repeat it.

    Use the form on the following page.

Page 10

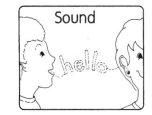

Color the circles to match the bottles

you tap to make your tune.

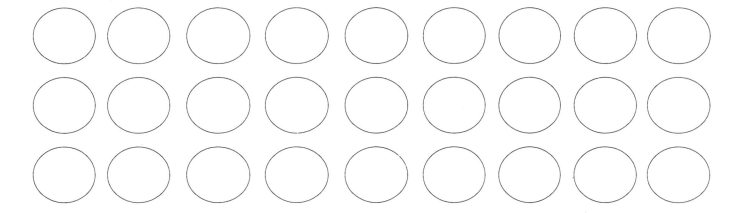

Now see if a friend can read the colors and repeat your tune.

　　　　　　　　　　Hands-On Science

Student: _____

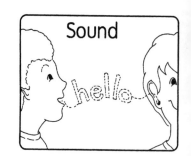
Sound

Date: _____

Dear Parents,

We have been studying about sound. Listen with your child to the sounds inside and outside your home. Discuss which are sounds of nature and which are man-made. Your child should complete this sheet and return it to school.

Sincerely,

What sounds do you hear in **nature**?	What sounds are **man-made**?

Hands-On Science

Foods

Foods

Objectives:

The student will learn:

1. Food can change from one form to another.
2. Food can develop mold.
3. Foods contain fat, starch, and vitamin C.
4. Texture, color, and smell play a strong role in the ability to taste food.

Materials to use with student lab books:

Page 1:
- whipping cream
- crackers
- baby food jars
- knife

Page 2:
- various foods, such as:
  tomato, banana,
  cheese, onion, lemon,
  and chocolate
- blindfold

Page 3:
- fruit gum drops
- blindfold

Page 4:
- colorless drinks, such as:
  sugar water, salty water,
  fizzy lemonade, and plain
  water
- small cups

Page 5:
- pieces of various foods
  (with and without fat)
- oil, water
- brown paper bag, water

Page 7:
- various fruit juices
- small jar
- indicator liquid *(see Helpful Hints)*
- white paper
- dropper
- ruler
- tape to mark jar

Page 9:
- small pieces of various foods
  (with and without starch)
- potato
- dish
- iodine
- dropper

Page 11:
- bread
- lettuce
- orange
- egg
- glass bowl

Helpful Hints:

Vitamin C indicator liquid (one gallon) can be made by mixing a heaping teaspoon of corn starch in a cup of cold water. Boil this mixture for two minutes. Put ten droppers full of this mixture into a gallon container of water. Add one dropper full of iodine. Cap the container and shake until mixture looks uniformly blue.

 Hands-On-Science

front cover

My Lab Book

Name _____

Date _____

Foods

- -

back cover

Three things I've learned about foods:

1. _____

2. _____

3. _____

Hands-On Science

Page 1

Foods

1. Fill 1/2 baby food jar with whipping cream.

2. Shake substance for about five minutes.

3. Record your observations.

_____

_____

_____

4. When substance changes into a creamy texture, spread onto salted crackers.

5. What new substance have you made? _____

- -

Page 2

Foods

1. Put on a blindfold.

   Taste each food and try to name it.

2. Record the foods you tasted.

   a. _____   d. _____

   b. _____   e. _____

   c. _____   f. _____

3. Some people will be able to tell the food by its texture.

   Can you think of a way to make it a taste-only test?

_____

_____

Page 3

Foods

1. Do a test with fruit gum drops.

2. Put on a blindfold.

3. Try to name each flavor and record the results.

<u>Color/Flavor Given</u>   <u>Color/Flavor Named</u>

1. _____   _____

2. _____   _____

3. _____   _____

4. _____   _____

4. People who have a cold sometimes say they cannot taste because
their nose is blocked. Try a test holding your nose and tasting.

Page 4

1. Observe the tray of colorless drinks.

2. Can you tell what is in each cup by looking? _____

3. Can you tell by smelling? _____

4. Can you tell by tasting? _____

5. Record the results of your taste test.

Drink Given   *Drink Named*

1. _____   _____

2. _____   _____

3. _____   _____

4. _____   _____

Foods

1. Spread a drop of oil on a brown paper bag.

2. Spread a drop of water alongside. Let it dry.

3. Hold up the paper bag to the light. Notice the difference in
    the two spots. Fat shows as a shiny, oily spot.

4. Observe the various pieces of food.

5. Which foods do you think have fat? _____

    _____

    _____

Page 6

Foods

1. Test the foods by rubbing each small piece
    onto the brown paper bag. Record your results.

Food	*Fat*	*No Fat*
_____	_____	_____
_____	_____	_____
_____	_____	_____
_____	_____	_____
_____	_____	_____

2. Which food tested had the most fat? _____

3. Which had the least fat? _____

Page 7

1. Mark a small jar about 1/2 inch (1.3 cm) from the bottom.

2. Pour indicator liquid into the jar to the mark.

3. Put the jar on white paper.

4. Test juice by adding it to the blue liquid one drop at a time.

5. Count the number of drops you put in.

   Stir the blue liquid as you add the drops.

6. Watch for the blue color of indicator liquid to disappear.

   When it is no longer blue, the test is over.

Page 8

1. Test the juices and record the results below.

   Be sure to rinse the jar and dropper before each new test.

   Juice   *Number of Drops*

   _____   _____

   _____   _____

   _____   _____

   _____   _____

   _____   _____

2. Which juice contained the most vitamin C?_____

   The least? _____

                                       Hands-On Science

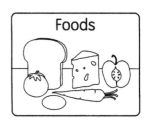

Foods

1.   Put a piece of potato in a dish.

2.   Drop a tiny bit of iodine on the potato.

3.   Does it turn either purple or black? _____

4.   If it turns purple or black, it contains starch.

5.   Test the various substances and complete the chart on the

      following page.

Be sure to clean the dish between each test item.

- -

Page 10
Substance to be Tested

*Does the
Substance
Contain
Starch?*

Foods

Substance to be Tested	Does the Substance Contain Starch?
_____	_____
_____	_____
_____	_____
_____	_____
_____	_____

What substance that you tested seemed to have the most starch?

_____

Foods

1. Place pieces of bread, lettuce, orange, and egg in a glass bowl near a window.

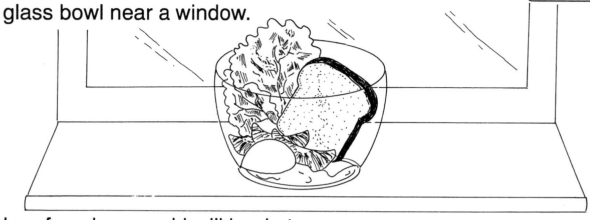

2. In a few days, mold will begin to grow.

3. Observe the mold growth and draw pictures of your observations on the following pages.

Foods

Bread After 2 Weeks	Bread After 4 Weeks

Hands-On Science

Page 13

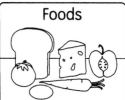

Foods

Lettuce After 2 Weeks	Lettuce After 4 Weeks

Page 14

Foods

Orange After 2 Weeks	Orange After 4 Weeks

Page 15

Egg After 2 Weeks	Egg After 4 Weeks

Page 16

1. Which food developed mold first? _____

2. How long did it take for the first mold to develop? _____

3. Which food developed mold last? _____

4. How long did it take for the last mold to develop?_____

5. Are all molds the same? _____

6. How are molds different? _____

_____

_____

Name _____

Date _____

Foods

Dear Parents,

We have been studying about foods. As a follow-up activity,
please have your child make a food book. You'll need magazines,
scissors, glue, and paper. Have your child select pictures of
foods he/she likes and dislikes to cut out. Glue the pictures to
sheets of paper. Have your child record his/her feelings about the
foods selected. You may need to help your child with the writing.
Staple or tie the pages together inside a cover. Have your child
bring his/her booklet to school to share with the class.

Sincerely,

How to make a food booklet:

1. Paste and write.

Add as many
pages as you need.

2. Make a cover.

Name the booklet.
Name the author.
Add a picture.

3. Bind the booklet.

staple or use yarn

Cold and Heat

Cold and Heat

Objectives:

The student will learn that:

1. When air is heated, the air atoms move further apart.
2. When air is cooled, the air atoms move closer together.
3. Heat changes the way food looks, tastes, and smells.
4. Light and dark coverings affect the rate of absorption of heat.
5. Water will condense when it meets with warmer air.
6. A thermometer is used to measure how hot and cold something is.

Materials to use with student lab books:

Page 1:
- three bowls with hot, cold, and warm water

Page 2:
- three bowls with hot, cold, and warm water
- ice cubes
- crushed ice
- stopwatch

Page 4:
- candle flame
- popcorn seed
- cooking oil
- test tube
- foil
- test tube holder (or wooden tongs)

Page 5:
- candle flame
- raisins
- test-tube
- foil
- test tube holder (or wooden tongs)

Page 6:
- pitcher of cold water
- three bottles
- black and white paper
- thermometer

Page 8:
- cold water
- ice cubes
- glass jar with lid

Page 9:
- water
- two ice cubes
- two glasses
- two thermometers

Attention:

All activities involving the use of a flame should be demonstrated by an adult.

Name _____

My Lab Book

Date _____

Cold and Heat

- -

Three things I've learned about cold and heat:

1. _____

2. _____

3. _____

Page 1

Cold and Heat

1. Put your left hand in the bowl of hot water, right

    hand in the bowl of cold. Wait one minute.

2. Put both hands in the warm water.

3. How does it feel? _____

4. How does your right hand feel? _____

5. How does your left hand feel? _____

6. Why? _____

    _____

    _____

- -

Page 2

Cold and Heat

1. Let's see who can make their ice cube melt the fastest.

    What can you do to make it melt?

2. Time the melting process.

    It took _____ minutes _____ seconds to melt.

3. Make your crushed ice melt.

4. Time the melting process.

    It took _____ minutes _____ seconds to melt.

5. Which ice melted more quickly, cubes or crushed?

    _____

6. Use your materials to complete the next page.

　　　　　　　　　　　　　　　　Hands-On Science

Page 3

Cold and Heat

1. Use the three pans of water: hot, warm and cold.

2. Which pan do you think will melt an ice cube the fastest?

   _____

3. Test and record the results. _____

   _____

   _____

   _____

   _____

- -

Page 4

Cold and Heat

1. Insert the test tube into the test tube holder. Put one

   corn seed and one drop of cooking oil into the test tube.

   Cover the top of the test tube with aluminum foil.

2. Place the test tube over a candle flame. Keep it one inch (2.5 cm)

   above the flame.

3. Rock the test tube back and forth.

4. After a few minutes, observe the changes.

5. What changes have occurred in the corn seed? _____

   _____

6. What did you do to help make the change? _____

Page 5

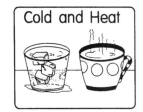
Cold and Heat

1. Put one raisin into a test tube.

   Cover the top of the test tube with aluminum foil.

2. Place the test tube over a candle flame, keeping it one inch

   above the flame.

3. Rock the test tube back and forth. Stop heating before the

   raisin turns black.

4. Record your observations. _____

   _____

   _____

   _____

- -

Page 6

Cold and Heat

1. Record the temperature of the pitcher of cold water.

   _____degrees

2. Fill three bottles with the cold water.

3. Wrap one bottle with black paper, one with white paper, and

   leave the third bottle unwrapped.

4. Place the bottles side by side in the warm sunshine.

5. Record your observations on the following page.

Cold and Heat

	Black Bottle	White Bottle	Plain Bottle
Beginning Temperature			
Temperature after 15 minutes			
Temperature after 30 minutes			
Temperature after 45 minutes			

Cold and Heat

1. Put some cold water in a glass jar.

2. Place some ice cubes in the water.

3. Put the lid on the jar. Shake it up.

4. What happens to the outside of the jar?

   _____

   _____

5. Where do you think the drops of water came from?

   _____

   _____

       Hands-On Science

Cold and Heat

1.   Measure the air temperature inside a glass with a

thermometer.

2 .   Also measure the temperature inside a glass of water. It

should be about the same as the air temperature. If not, let

the water stand a while.

3.   Find two ice cubes that are the same size.

4.   Put one ice cube into the empty glass, the other into the

glass of water.

5.   Answer the questions on the following page.

- -

Cold and Heat

1.   Which ice cube melts the fastest? _____

_____

2.   How can you make an ice cube melt faster in water?

_____

3.   Will stirring the water make a difference? _____

4.   Will an ice cube melt faster in warmer water?_____

                                                           Hands-On Science

Student: _____

Date: _____

Dear Parents,

We have been studying about cold and heat. Your child will need a balloon and tape measure for the following activity. Please have your child return this completed sheet to school.

1. Blow up a balloon and tie it tightly so no air can escape.

2. Measure around the balloon at the biggest part. The original size of the balloon is _____ inches/centimeters.

3. Place the balloon in the refrigerator for one hour.

4. What is the size of the balloon after being in the refrigerator one hour? _____ inches/centimeters

5. Does air take up more room when it is cold or warm? _____

6. Do not do this next experiment because the balloon would probably melt, but if you could heat the air inside the balloon, do you think it would take up more space? _____ What might happen to the balloon? _____

_____

Sincerely,

Sink and Float

Sink and Float

Objectives:

The student will learn that:

1. Generally, heavy things sink and light things float.
2. Sponges, cloth, and paper absorb water.
3. Water has weight and water weight helps things float.

Materials to use with student lab books:

Page 1:
- collection of small sinking and floating objects: pencil, key, marble, plastic objects, eraser, cork, and small toy figures
- tray or box lids to label "sink" and "float"
- large container of water

Page 3:
- collection of various weights of materials: pieces of card board, wax paper, etc.
- paper towel
- sponge
- cloth
- tagboard
- stopwatch
- water

Page 4:
- collection of objects
- clay (oil base)
- foil

Page 6:
- marble
- two large containers of water
- salt

Page 7:
- shelled hard-boiled egg
- two glasses
- salt
- water

Page 8:
- collection of objects
- two large containers of water
- cooking oil
- corn syrup

Helpful Hints:

Before you begin, be sure the children understand the difference between sinking and floating. For a salt water solution, you'll need about three pounds of salt to one gallon of water.

My Lab Book

Name _____

Date _____

Sink and Float

- -

Three things I've learned about sinking and floating:

1. _____

2. _____

3. _____

Hands-On Science

Page 1

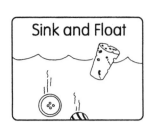

Sink and Float

1. Examine the objects.

   Which do <u>you think</u> will float?   Which do <u>you think</u> will sink?

   _____   _____

   _____   _____

   _____   _____

   _____   _____

2. Test each object to see if it sinks or floats.

3. Separate objects on the "sink" and "float" tray.

4. Record your findings on the following page.

- -

Page 2

Sink and Float

<u>Item</u>   <u>Sink</u>   <u>Float</u>

_____   _____   _____

_____   _____   _____

_____   _____   _____

_____   _____   _____

_____   _____   _____

_____   _____   _____

_____   _____   _____

                                       Hands-On Science

Page 3

Sink and Float

1. Drop each item, one at a time, in the water and record the time it takes for each to sink.

Item	Time
_____	_____
_____	_____
_____	_____
_____	_____
_____	_____

Page 4

Sink and Float

1. Let's see if you can make some of the objects that float, sink. For example, put something that sinks on something that floats.

2. Now see if you can make some of the objects that sink, float. For example, can you find a way to make clay float?

    _____

3. Experiment with clay and aluminum foil. Find ways to make them sink and float.

4. Record your findings on the following page.

Page 5

Sink and Float

1.	Under what conditions did the clay sink?

	_____

2.	Under what conditions did the clay float?

	_____

3.	Under what conditions did the foil sink?

	_____

4.	Under what conditions did the foil float?

	_____

- -

Page 6

Sink and Float

1.	Let's compare sinking and floating in two different

	liquids--**plain** water and **salt** water.

2.	How much salt do you think is needed to get a marble,

	which sank in plain water, to float in salt water?

	_____

3.	Make a salt-water solution by adding one handful of salt at a

	time to a container of water.

4.	Test the marble after each handful of salt is added.

5.	How many handfuls of salt did it take to make the marble

	float? _____

Page 7

Sink and Float

1.   Fill two glasses 1/2 full of water.

2.   Dissolve salt in one glass.

3.   Drop a shelled hard-boiled egg into the plain water.

     What happens?_____

4.   Now drop the egg into the salt water.

     What happens?_____

5.   Slowly pour plain water down the side of the glass with salt

     water so that there is a layer of plain water on top. Now

     what happens to the egg?_____

     Why? _____

     _____

- -

Page 8

Sink and Float

1.   Try floating objects in two more different liquids--
   water with cooking oil added and water with corn
   syrup added.

2.   Record your findings below.

Item			*Item*		
In Oil	Sink	Float	**In Syrup**	Sink	Float

Student: _____

Date: _____

Sink and Float

Dear Parents,

We have performed several sink and float experiments. As a follow-up to what we've done in class, please help your child gather various objects and test whether they sink or float in different water solutions. Make these solutions by adding sugar, baking soda, salt or other substances to water. Record your results on the chart below and return it to school.

Water with _____			Water with _____		
Item	**Sink**	**Float**	Item	**Sink**	**Float**

Hands-On-Science

Magnets

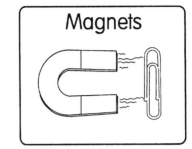
Objectives:

The student will learn that:
1. Magnets attract some metals, but not all.
2. Magnets attract and repel each other.
3. Magnets may have different shapes.
4. Permanent magnets can be used to make temporary magnets.
5. Magnets are strongest at their poles.
6. Magnets can be used as compasses.
7. Some magnets are stronger than others.

Materials to use with student lab books:

Page 1:
- horseshoe and bar magnets

Page 2:
- magnet
- collection of objects: some which are and some which are not attracted to magnets

Page 3:
- magnet
- one tablespoon of iron filings
- two tablespoons of salt

Page 4:
- magnet
- paper clip

Page 6:
- magnet
- large iron nail
- straight pins

Page 7:
- magnets (different kinds)
- white paper
- iron filings

Page 8:
- magnet
- margarine tub
- needle
- cork or piece of styrofoam
- water
- compass

Page 9:
- two bar magnets
- string

Page 10:
- magnet
- paper clip
- margarine tub
- iron filings
- plastic glass
- water

Helpful Hints:

Handle magnets with care. Dropping them will cause magnets to become weaker.
Store magnets with a nail across poles or with opposite poles together.

front cover

My Lab Book

Name _____

Date _____

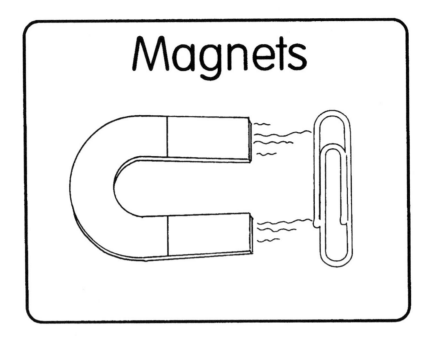

Magnets

- -

back cover

Three things I've learned about magnets:

1. _____

2. _____

3. _____

52

Page 1

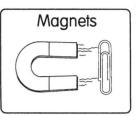

Draw a horseshoe magnet. Label the poles.	Draw a bar magnet. Label the poles.

Page 2

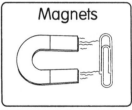

Draw six things that **are** attracted to the magnet.	Draw six things **not** attracted to the magnet.

Page 3

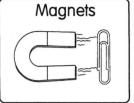

1.   Put one tablespoon of iron filings and two tablespoons of salt into a jar.

2.   How can you separate the filings from the salt? _____

_____

3.   Draw a picture to show how.

- -

Page 4

1.   Use the following page to do this experiment.

2.   Put the paper clip on the top line.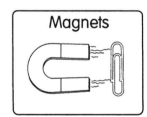

3.   Line up a pole of the magnet with the clip.

4.   Slowly bring the magnet near the clip.

5.   Stop when the magnet moves the clip.

6.   How many lines did it take? _____

Page 5

_____

_____

_____

_____

_____

_____

_____

_____

- -

Page 6

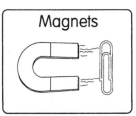

Magnets

1.   Take a large iron nail.

2.   Touch it to some pins to see if it attracts them.

3.   Stroke the whole nail with the magnet always in one
     direction, 35 times.

4.   Touch the nail to the pins again.

     What happened?

     _____

     _____

Page 7

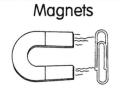

1.   Place a bar magnet on the table.

2.   Lay white paper over it.

3.   Sprinkle iron filings on the paper.

4.   Draw a picture showing what you see.

5.   Try the experiment with other magnets.

Page 8

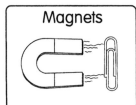

1.   Fill a container to the brim with water.

2.   Magnetize a needle. (Read page 6 if you don't remember how to do this.)

3.   Scratch a narrow groove in a cork.

4.   Lay the needle in the groove.

5.   Place the cork and needle on the water.

6.   In which direction does it point? _____

7.   Compare the results with the compass.

8.   Draw a picture of your experiment.

Page 9

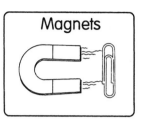
Magnets

1. Tie a string around the middle of one bar magnet.

2. Bring one end of the other bar magnet toward the magnet

    with the string.

    What happened? _____

    _____

3. Try the other end.

    What happened? _____

    _____

- -

Page 10

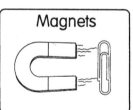
Magnets

1. Put some water into a container.

2. Drop in a paper clip.

3. Put the magnet into the water.

4. Does the magnet attract through the water? _____

5. Place a teaspoon of iron filings into a plastic glass.

    Add water and stir.

6. Move the magnet around the outside of the glass.

7. Draw a picture on the back of this page showing what happens.

Student:_____

Date:_____

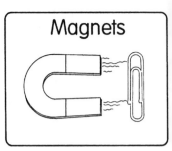
Dear Parents,

We have been studying about magnets. Your child has learned that magnets are attracted to some objects and are not attracted to others. Please help him/her collect objects to bring to school to test with a magnet. Have your child predict which of the objects will be attracted by a magnet and which objects will not. Help your child write the predictions below. We will test the objects at school with a magnet. All objects will be returned.

Sincerely,

Predict what might happen when using a magnet:	
These objects will be attracted.	**These objects will not be attracted.**
_____	_____
_____	_____
_____	_____
_____	_____
_____	_____
_____	_____

Hands-On-Science

Bubbles and Air

Objectives:

The student will learn that:
1. Air cannot be seen, but we can see what air does.
2. Air has weight and pressure and takes up space.
3. Bubbles have air inside.
4. Light passing through a bubble changes color.
5. Bubbles tend to occupy the smallest area.

Materials to use with student lab books:

Page 1:
• balloon
• margarine tub
• drinking straw
• water

Page 2:
• two balloons
• yardstick
• string
• tape

Page 3:
• paper towel
• plastic glass
• tape
• large open container of water

Page 4:
• plastic glass
• piece of cardboard
• water
• tub

Page 5:
• bubble mix
• plastic glass
• drinking straw

Page 6:
• bubble mix
• drinking straw

Page 7:
• pan with bubble mix
• two drinking straws
• three-foot (91.5 cm) piece of string

Page 8:
• bubble mix
• plastic glass
• food coloring
• pipe cleaner
• white paper

Helpful Hints:

When working with bubbles, keep hands and all surfaces soapy. Bubbles burst when they touch something dry. The size of the bubble does not depend on how hard you blow, rather the way you blow. Shape your mouth into an "O." A sudden burst of air blows small bubbles; a steady breath blows larger bubbles.

Bubble mix can be made by combining one cup of dishwashing soap, sixteen cups of water, and one tablespoon of glycerine. You may substitute sugar or corn syrup for glycerine. Let solution sit for one day.

front cover

My Lab Book

Name _____

Date _____

Bubbles and Air

- -

back cover

Three things I've learned about bubbles and air:

1. _____

2. _____

3. _____

60

Page 1

1. Blow up a balloon.

2. Let the air out.

3. Can you see the air? _____

4. Blow up the balloon again.

5. Let the air out in a margarine tub of water.

6. What do you see? _____

_____

7. Put a straw in the water. Blow gently. What do you see?

_____

_____

Page 2

1. Tie a string around the middle of a yardstick and

   tape it to a doorway or another place.

2. Blow up two balloons the same size.

3. Tape a balloon to each end of the yardstick so that the stick

   is balanced.

4. Pop one balloon. What happens?

_____

_____

5. Does air have weight? _____

Hands-On Science

Bubbles and Air

1.   Crumple a paper towel.

2.   Put it into a plastic glass.

3.   Tape it in place at the bottom of the glass.

4.   Tip the glass upside down, and put it into a tub of water.

5.   Count to 10 and take the glass out.

6.   Why didn't the towel get wet? _____

       _____

7.   Does air take up space? _____

- -

Page 4

Bubbles and Air

1.   Put some water in a glass.

2.   Slide cardboard over the top of the glass making sure there

       are no bubbles of air in the glass.

3.   Hold cardboard tight against the glass and turn the glass

       upside down (over a tub).

4.   Take your hand away. What happens? _____

       _____

       _____

       _____

       Hands-On Science

Page 5

Bubbles and Air

1. Pour 1/2 a glass of bubble mix.

2. Soap the glass inside and out.

3. Estimate how many bubbles you can blow in the glass with

    a straw. _____

4. Blow gently. Did you estimate more or less? _____

5. Gently blow 1 bubble.

    Estimate how high you think it will go. _____

6. Estimate how far you can count before a bubble breaks:

    a big bubble _____ a small bubble _____

Page 6

Bubbles and Air

1. Soap the surface of a table area with the bubble mix.

2. Lean over the table and using a straw, gently blow bubbles.

3. Blow one large bubble. Examine the bubble.

4. What is inside the bubble? _____

5. Does the bubble move? _____

6. What shape is it? _____

7. Can you see colors in your bubble? _____

8. Soap the straw. Push it gently through the bubble and blow

    another bubble. Can you do it again? _____

Page 7

1. Run a piece of string through 2 straws.

2. Tie the string to make a rectangle.

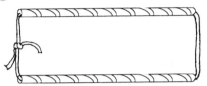

3. Dip the rectangle in a pan with bubble mix.

4. Lift it out to form a rectangular window.

5. Pull it upward to form a bubble.

6. Turn it upside down.

7. Close off the bubble by bringing the straws together.

8. Is the bubble shaped like a rectangle? _____

Page 8

1. Put bubble mix in a plastic glass.

2. Add food coloring to your mix.

3. Make a circle out of one end of a pipe cleaner. Dip the circle

   in the bubble mix. Blow bubbles.

4. Blow some bubbles over a piece of white paper.

   What happens when the bubbles burst?

   _____

   _____

   _____

Student: _____

Date: _____

Bubbles and Air

Dear Parents,

We have been studying about bubbles and air. Ask your child to explain what he/she has learned. Brainstorm with your child to create a list of things that have bubbles. Return the completed list to school.

Sincerely,

Things that have bubbles:

1. _____

2. _____

3. _____

4. _____

5. _____

6. _____

7. _____

8. _____

 Hands-On-Science

Hands-On-Science

Plants

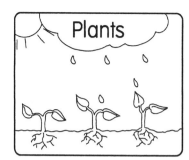

Objectives:

The student will learn:

1. The characteristics of green plants.
2. The needs of plants - water and light.
3. The parts of plants and seeds.
4. The function of plant parts.
5. The process of growth from seeds.

Materials to use with student lab books:

Page 1:
• bird seed
• scotch tape

Page 2:
• small zip-lock baggie
• stapler
• paper towel
• dropper
• magnifying glass
• seeds

Page 3:
• two lima bean seeds
• two cups of soil

Page 7:
• soaked lima bean seeds
• plastic glass
• paper towels
• magnifying glass

Page 10:
• soaked and dry, bean and corn seeds

Page 11:
• lima bean seed
• cup of soil

Page 12:
• measuring tape

Helpful Hints:

Seeds should be soaked at least one hour before dissecting.

My Lab Book

Name _____

Date _____

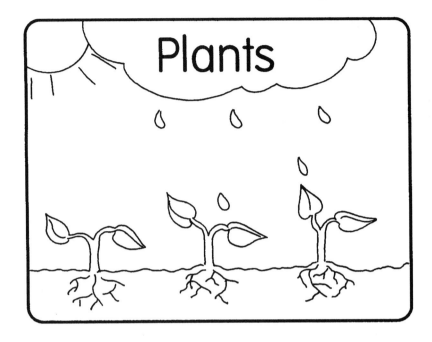

Plants

- -

Three things I've learned about plants:

1. _____

2. _____

3. _____

Page 1

1. Sort the bird seed into groups.

2. Tape one of each type of seed here.

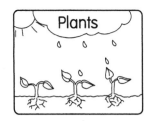

Page 2

1. Make a baggie garden. Fold a paper towel and fit it into the baggie. Put a row of staples about an inch (2.5 cm) from the bottom. Put a few seeds in the baggie. Water the seeds with the dropper and hang the baggie up. Do not close the top of the bag.

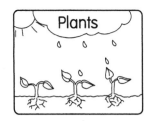

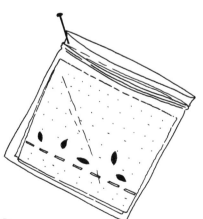

2. In a few days, observe your seeds with a magnifying glass. Draw a picture of the seeds in your baggie garden on the back of this page.

   Label: roots, root hairs, stems, and leaves.

  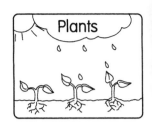

1.   Plant a seed in each of two cups of soil.

2.   Place one cup in sunlight and the other in a dark place.

3.   Water each plant daily.

4.   Observe both plants and draw pictures of your experiment

     on the following pages.

- -

Page 4 # After 5 Days

In The Dark	In The Light

Page 5

After 10 Days

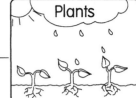
Plants

In The Dark	**In The Light**

Page 6

After 15 Days

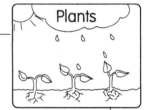
Plants

In The Dark	**In The Light**

                   Hands-On Science

Page 7

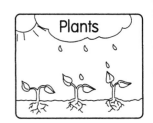
1. Put a wet paper towel around the inside of a plastic glass.

2. Crumple another towel in the middle of the glass to hold the seeds and the wet towel in place.

3. Put two or three soaked seeds between the paper and glass. Place the seeds in different positions.

4. In a few days examine the roots with your magnifying glass. Draw pictures of the roots on the following page.

- -

Page 8

Draw the Roots

5 Days	10 Days	15 Days

Page 9

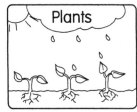

1. Did the position of the seeds in your plastic glass make a difference in the way the stems and roots grew? _____

2. Turn the glass on its side. In a few days, observe your plant. Which way are the plants and roots growing now?

   _____

3. What is your conclusion? _____

   _____

   _____

   _____

- -

Page 10

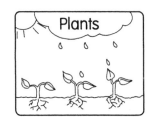

1. Remove the seed coats from the soaked bean and corn seeds.

2. Can you remove the seed coat from dry seeds?

3. Use your thumb nail to dissect seeds.

4. Can you find the embryo plant? _____

5. Draw a picture of the dissected seeds.

   Label: seed covering, embryo plant.

Page 11

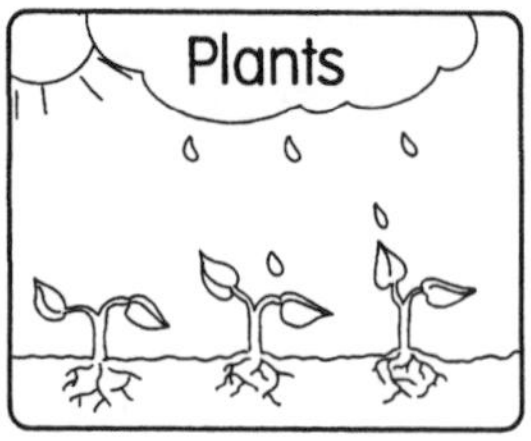

1. Plant a lima bean seed in a cup of soil.

2. Complete the chart below.

Date

_____ I planted my seed.

_____ My seed sprouted.

_____ My plant had flowers.

_____ My plant produced pods.

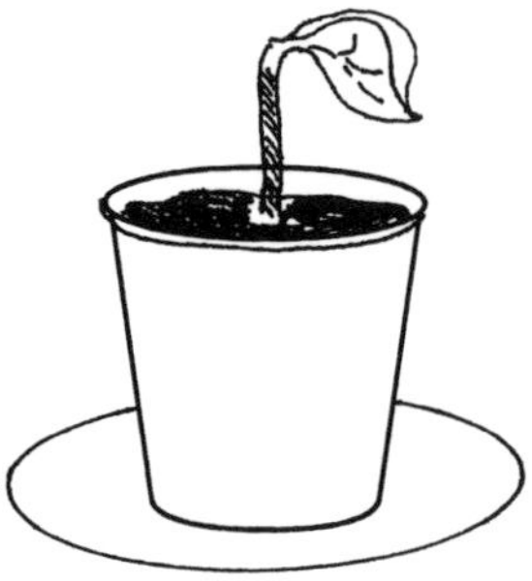

3. Things I did to take care of my plant.

_____

_____

Page 12   # Growth Graph

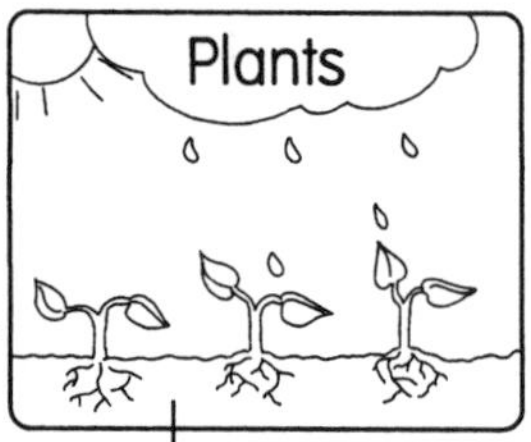

Measure your lima bean plant and complete the graph.

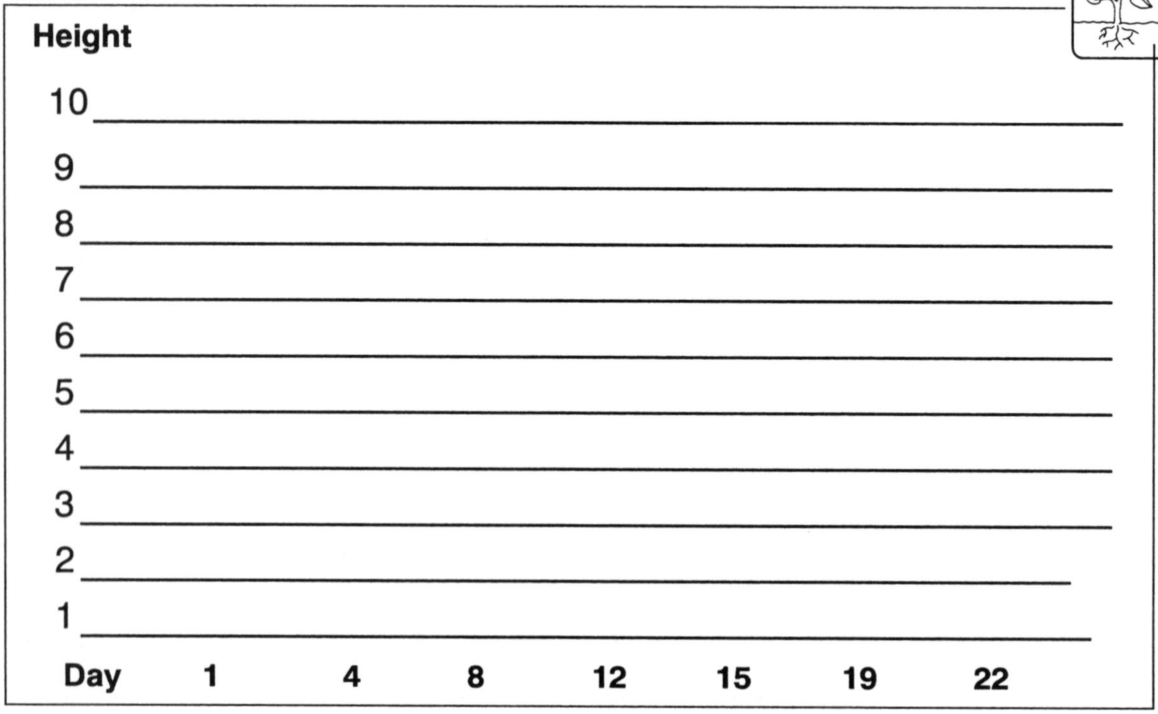

Height

10	
9	
8	
7	
6	
5	
4	
3	
2	
1	
Day	1 4 8 12 15 19 22

Student: _____

Date: _____

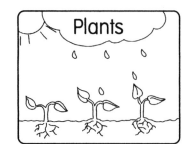

Plants

Dear Parents,

We have been studying about plants. Please help your child plant

a seed (from any fruit or vegetable with seeds) in a cup of soil or

in the ground. He/she should care for and observe the plant and

fill in the chart below. Return the completed chart to school.

Type of seed	Date planted
Draw pictures of your plant.	

After 5 days	After 10 days	After 15 days

Hands-On-Science

Mealworms and Snails

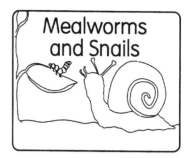

Objectives:

The student will learn:
1. To be aware of similarities and differences in small living things.
2. To gain experience in observing and recording behavior and characteristics of living things.

Materials to use with student lab books:

Page 1:
- mealworm
- box lid
- spoon
- hand lens

Page 3:
- mealworms
- box lid
- piece of cardboard
- book
- piece of white and piece of black paper

Page 4:
- two mealworms
- clear drinking straw
- ice cube
- rough-surfaced paper towel

Page 5:
- mealworm
- dropper
- wax paper
- water
- vinegar and samples of other strong odors, such as: oil of cloves, peppermint, and vanilla
- cotton balls

Page 6:
- mealworm
- stopwatch

Page 7:
- snail
- pie pan
- spoon
- hand lens

Page 9:
- snail

Page 10:
- snail
- piece of black paper

Page 12:
- snail
- bits of different foods
- lettuce
- hand lens
- vinegar and other odors
- dropper
- cotton ball

Helpful Hints:

Students should be able to bring in snails from their own backyards. Mealworms can be inexpensively purchased in a store that sells worms for fishing. They should be refrigerated (with a piece of apple for moisture) until ready to use. If you wish to grow your own mealworms, keep the larva at room temperature. They will be active and busy eating for a while and then will slow down to a resting pupa. A black, fat and completely harmless beetle will emerge. It will lay eggs and then die. Eggs will hatch into mealworms. The entire process requires several weeks.

 Hands-On-Science

Name _____

My Lab Book

Date _____

Mealworms and Snails

- -

Three things I've learned about mealworms and snails:

1. _____

2. _____

3. _____

Page 1

Mealworms and Snails

1. Put a mealworm in an upturned box lid.

2. Use a spoon to move it where you want.

3. Examine the mealworm with your hand lens.

4. How many legs does it have? _____

5. How many feelers does it have on its head? _____

6. Does it have a mouth? _____

7. Does it have eyes? _____

8. What is on its tail end? _____

9. How many body segments does it have? _____

- -

Page 2

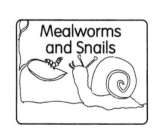

Mealworms and Snails

1. Draw a mealworm.

2. Label its parts:

   body segments

   head

   legs

   feelers

   tail

Hands-On Science

Page 3

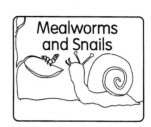
Mealworms and Snails

1. Put a few mealworms in the box lid.

2. Can you tell them apart? _____

3. Put them in the middle of an incline.

   (Lean a piece of cardboard on a book.)

4. Will they crawl up or down? _____

5. Place a piece of black paper beside a piece of white paper.

   Put the mealworms in the middle.

6. Do they like the white or the black color? _____

_ _

Page 4

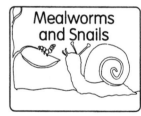
Mealworms and Snails

1. Put two mealworms into a drinking straw, one at each end.

2. What happens when they meet? _____

3. Put an ice cube near a mealworm.

4. Does it move towards or away from the ice? _____

5. Put a mealworm on a smooth desk. Put a rough-surfaced

   paper towel beside the mealworm.

6. Does it like the rough or the smooth surface? _____

Page 5

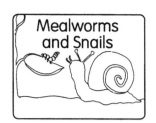
Mealworms and Snails

1. Put a few drops of water on a piece of wax paper.

2. Put a mealworm near the water.

3. Observe the mealworm for five minutes.

4. Does the mealworm go into the water? _____

5. Put a few drops of vinegar on a cotton ball.

6. Place it near a mealworm. What happens?

    _____

7. Experiment with other odors. Do you think a mealworm has

    a sense of smell? _____

Page 6

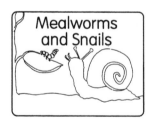
Mealworms and Snails

Observe a mealworm. Draw a line to show how far the mealworm can go in one minute.

Start

here

  X

Mealworms
and Snails

1. Put a snail in a pie pan. Use a spoon to move it where you want.

2. With your hand lens examine the snail.

3. How does it move? _____

    _____

    _____

4. Can you find its head? _____

5. Can you find its eyes? _____

6. Can you find its feelers? _____

- -

Page 8

Mealworms
and Snails

1. Draw a snail.
2. Label its parts: head, legs, shell, feelers, and eyes.

Page 9

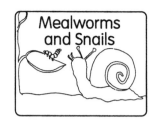
Mealworms
and Snails

1. How many feelers do you see on the snail's head?

2. Which feelers seem to have eyes?

    the long ones_____   the short ones _____

3. Gently touch the two longer feelers.

4. Gently touch the two shorter feelers.

5. Which ones seem to be used for feeling? _____

6. See how close you can come before the feelers move.

    Can you make the two longer feelers move in different

    directions? _____

Page 10

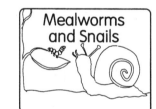
Mealworms
and Snails

1. Tap the snail's shell gently.

2. What happens? _____

    _____

3. Put the snail upside down.

4. Can it right itself? _____

5. Can you make the snail go fast without hurting it? _____

6. Put the snail on a piece of black paper.

    Observe the silver trail it makes.

7. Draw a picture of the snail and its trail on the following page.

                                       Hands-On Science

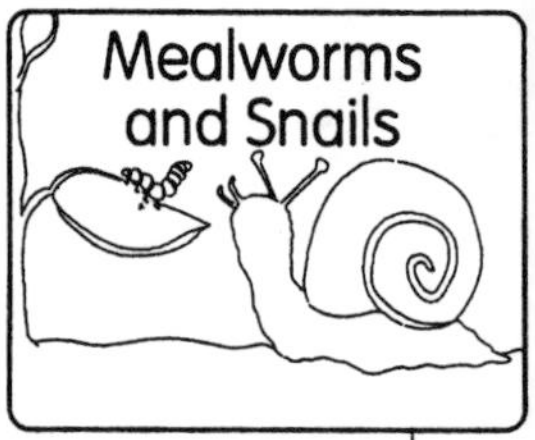

Mealworms and Snails

Snail Trail

Mealworms and Snails

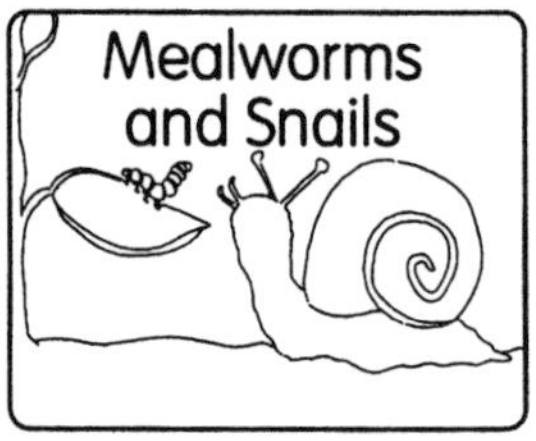

1. Circle your snail with bits of different kinds of food.

2. Which food does the snail go to first? _____

3. Give the snail some lettuce to eat.

4. Use your hand lens to watch its mouth parts.

5. Put a few drops of vinegar on a cotton ball.

6. Place it near the snail. What happens? _____

    _____

7. Experiment with other odors.

    Do you think the snail has a sense of smell? _____

Student: _____

Date: _____

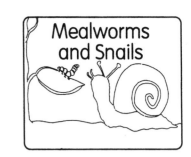

Mealworms and Snails

Dear Parents,

We have been studying about mealworms and snails. Help your child fill in the form below comparing the similarities and differences of these two small creatures.

Sincerely,

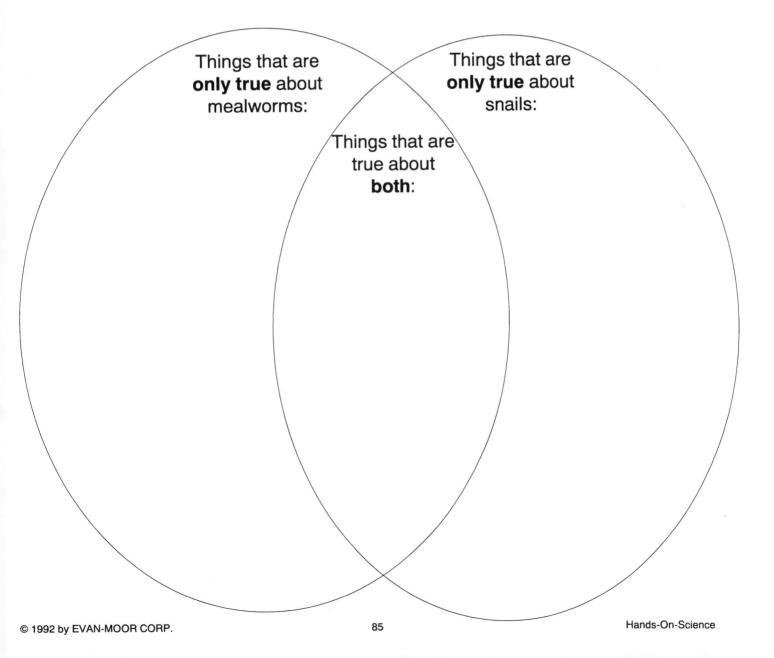

Things that are **only true** about mealworms:

Things that are **only true** about snails:

Things that are true about **both**:

Hands-On-Science

Hands-On-Science

Color

Objectives:

The student will learn that:
1. Primary colors mix to create new colors.
2. Light contains many colors.
3. Water or glass can bend light so that we can see the rainbow colors.

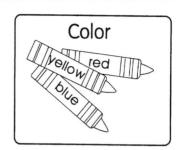

Color
yellow red
blue

Materials to use with student lab books:

Page 1:
• red, yellow, and blue crayons

Page 2:
• red, yellow, and blue crayons

Page 3:
• red, yellow, and blue food coloring
• dropper
• wax paper
• toothpick
• three plastic glasses half full of water

Page 4:
• red and blue food coloring
• wax paper
• toothpick
• plastic glass half full of water
• white paper towel

Page 5:
• food coloring

Page 6:
• squares of white and colored paper (red, yellow, blue)
• cellophane filters-red, yellow and blue

Page 7:
• cellophane filters
• crayons

Page 8:
• pie pan half filled with water
• mirror
• white paper

Page 9:
• glass of water

Page 10:
• crayons

Helpful Hints:

Colored cellophane may be purchased at crafts stores on a roll in a variety of colors. Cut into 6" x 8" (15 x 20.5 cm) pieces. Encase edges in masking tape for ease in handling and to prevent tearing. Fold cellophane filters for more intense colors.

Name _____

My Lab Book

Date _____

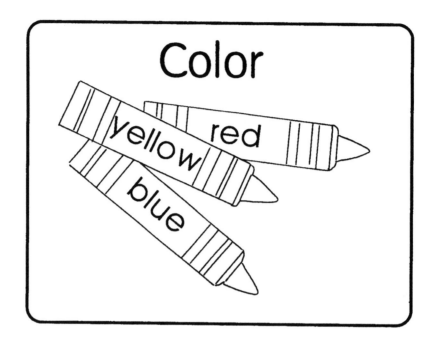

Color

yellow red

blue

- -

Three things I've learned about colors:

1. _____

2. _____

3. _____

Page 1

Use the side of a crayon and lightly rub one red line, one yellow line, and one blue line on your paper by connecting the O's.

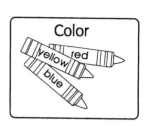

```
          X           X           X

    O                                   O



    O                                   O



    O                                   O

         X           X           X
```

Page 2

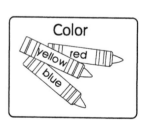

1. Go back to page 1 and using the same three crayons, rub three lines up and down connecting the X's.

2. What colors do you see where the lines cross?

_____   _____   _____

Hands-On Science

Page 3

1. Fill three plastic glasses half full of water.

2. Make each glass a different color by putting in two drops of red, yellow, or blue food coloring.

3. Take two drops from the red glass and two drops from the yellow glass and put them on a piece of wax paper. Mix with a toothpick.

4. Do the same with the red and blue glasses and the blue and yellow glasses.

5. What new colors did you mix?

_____ _____ _____

Page 4

Color

1. Put one drop of red food coloring and one drop of blue on wax paper. Mix with a toothpick.

2. Drop a dot of the mixture in the middle of a paper towel strip.

3. Hold the strip in a plastic glass that is about half full of water. The colored dot should be just above the water level.

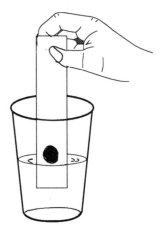

4. Hold for a couple of minutes.

5. Answer the questions on the following page.

Page 5

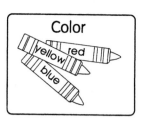

1. What happens to the color as water is

    soaked up past the colored dot?

    _____

2. How many colors appear as the colored dot spreads out?

    _____

3. Experiment with three colors. Record your findings below.

    _____

    _____

    _____

    _____

- -

Page 6

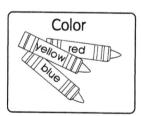

1. Put some white paper on a desk top.

2. Look at the paper through each cellophane filter.

    What colors do you see? _____ _____ _____

3. Try the same experiment using colored papers.

    What colors do you see?

• red paper with a red filter_____	• yellow paper with a red filter_____	• blue paper with a red filter_____
• red paper with a yellow filter_____	• yellow paper with a yellow filter_____	• blue paper with a yellow filter_____
• red paper with a blue filter_____	• yellow paper with a blue filter_____	• blue paper with a blue filter_____

Page 7

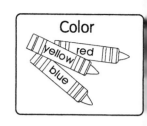

1. Look at these pictures through each of the color filters.

2. Try putting two filters together and watch the pictures change.

3. Now color the pictures with crayons and look at them through the filters. What changes have you created?

Page 8

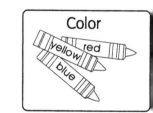

1. Place pan of water in the sun.

2. With the mirror facing the sun, hold the mirror upright against the pan's inside rim.

3. Slowly tip back the mirror.
   Sunlight must strike the mirror below the water's surface.

4. Point the mirror toward a large sheet of white paper.

5. What colors do you see on the wall? _____

   _____

6. What happens to the colors if you stir the water lightly?

   _____

1. Place a full glass of water on a window ledge in the bright sunlight.

2. Allow the glass to hang a little over the edge of the window ledge.

3. Find a rainbow of colors on the floor.

4. On the following page, use your crayons to make the rainbow.

- -

Page 10   # My Rainbow

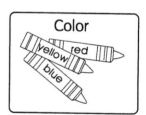

1. What color is at the top of the rainbow? _____

2. What color is at the bottom? _____

                     Hands-On Science

Student: _____

Date: _____

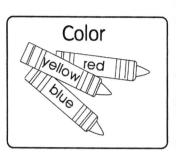

Color

Dear Parents,

We have been experimenting in class with the three basic colors: red, yellow and blue. You can continue to explore how color works with your child by doing the following experiment at home. Record the results on the attached color wheel form.

      1. Mix up bowls of red (cherry), yellow (lemon), and blue (blueberry) flavored gelatin. Have your child record these colors on the color wheel with crayons.

      2. Mix some yellow and red gelatin in a glass.
         Record the result on the color wheel.

      3. Mix some yellow and blue gelatin in a glass.
         Record the result.

      4. Mix some red and blue gelatin in a glass.
         Record the result.

Chill the gelatin and enjoy the results of your experiment.
Return the completed form to school.

Sincerely,

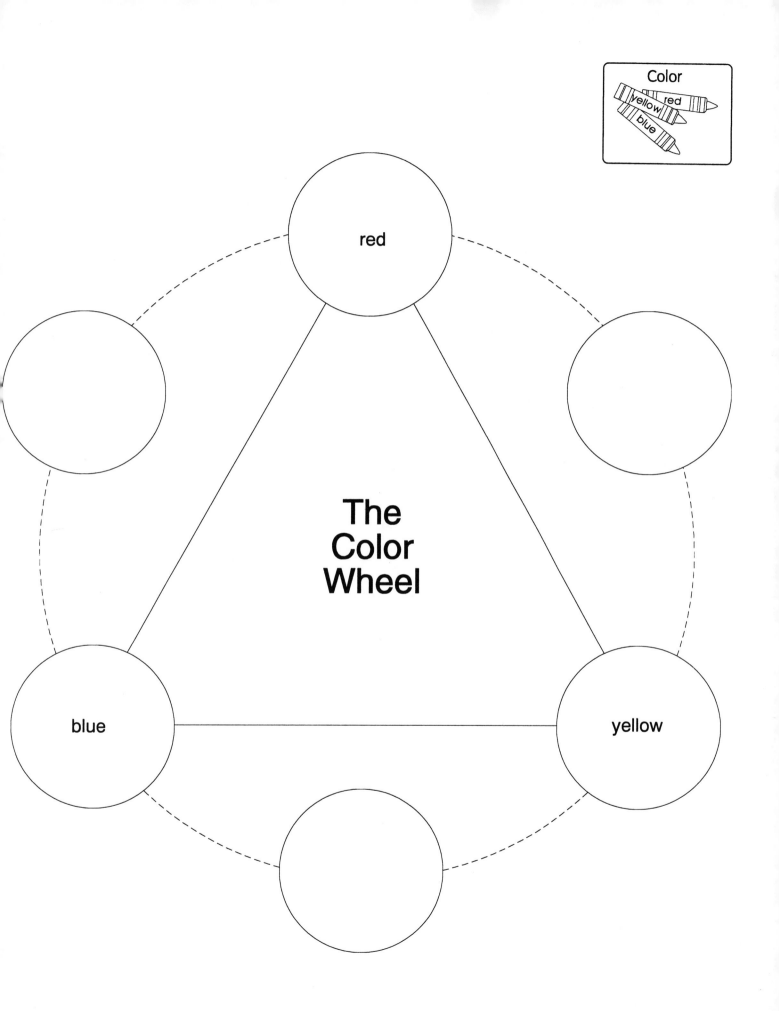

The Color Wheel

red

blue

yellow

Color

Hands-On Science

Resources

Brown, Sam Ed. **Bubbles, Rainbows, and Worms.** Maryland: Gryphom House, Inc., 1981.

Daniel, Charlie and Becky. **I Wonder**. Illinois: Good Apple, Inc., 1980.

De Bruin, Jerry. **Creative, Hands-On Science Experiments**. Illinois: Good Apple, Inc., 1980.

Gega, Peter C. **Science in Elementary Education**: Fifth Edition. New York: John Wiley & Sons, Inc., 1986.

Hans Jurgen Press. **Simple Science Experiments**. Germany: Otto Maier Verlag Ravensburg, 1967.

Knight, Michael E. and Terry L. Graham. **The Leaves Are Falling In Rainbows**. Atlanta, Georgia: Humanics Limited, 1984.

Mallinson, George G. **Science**. New Jersey: Silver Burdett Co., 1985.

McGraw-Hill. **Sink or Float**. New York: Webster Division, 1971.

Neal, Charles D. **Sound**. Sacramento: California State Department of Education, 1967.

Richards, Roy and Doug Kincaid. **Ourselves**. London: Macdonald & Co. Ltd., 1981.

Strongin, Herb. **Science On A Shoestring**. California: Addison-Wesley Publishing Company, 1985.

Zinkgraf, June and Toni Bauman. **Winter Wonders**. Illinois: Good Apple, Inc., 1978.